CARTOGRAPHIES

Map of the World, 1682

CARTOGRAPHIES

POEMS BY

ELEANOR SWANSON

SHANTI ARTS PUBLISHING

BRUNSWICK, MAINE

CARTOGRAPHIES

Published by Shanti Arts Publishing

Interior and cover design by Shanti Arts Designs

Shanti Arts LLC
193 Hillside Road
Brunswick, Maine 04011
shantiarts.com

Cover image: *World Map*, 1689. Produced
in Amsterdam using copper engraving.

ISBN: 978-1-971191-03-4 (softcover)

Library of Congress Control Number: 2026935371

for Bud

Contents

V. "A map says to you, 'Read me carefully, follow me closely, doubt me not.' It says, 'I am the earth in the palm of your hand. Without me, you are alone and lost.'" —Beryl Markham, *West with the Wind*

VI. *How do we map our lives? It is also called "way finding." A human needs to feel in place. Thematic cartography deconstructs our perceptions of literal maps and speaks to us in powerful ways.*

Acknowledgments

My thanks to the editors of the publications in which these poems
first appeared:

The American Journal of Poetry: "Festival at Shiprock" and
    "Mapping Middle Earth"

Beyond Words Literary Magazine: "Water Is the Driving Force
    of All Nature"

Bosque Journal: "Marie Tharp's Cartography of the Ocean Floor"

Free Trade Journal: "His Map"

Hamilton Stone Review: "Bombed-Out Cities"; "Drafting My
    Desire"; and "Geography: An Illusion"

Inverted Syntax: "I Map My Life's Tattoo" and "Literary Maps"

Unlikely Stories: "Delicate Indeed. Yet So Fragile" and "Public
    Discourse"

Abundant gratitude to Christine Cote, editor and publisher of
Shanti Arts Press, who accepted my *Cartographies* manuscript and
who has mentored me as we have worked together to release
this collection. Thanks as well to my husband Robert (Bud)
Fogerty who has been my patient and intuitive partner for many
years. As I write this, I think with affection of my family, friends,
and fellow poets and writers to whom I am grateful.

I write especially in memoriam and to honor a great and kind
man—activist, fellow poet, dancer, and more. He left this world
October 2025, and he now lives in abundant love.
                    I miss him—Wayne A. Gilbert.

"A map provides no answers. . . . Sometimes a map speaks in terms of physical geography, but just as often it muses on the jagged terrain of the heart, the distant vistas of memory, or the fantastic landscapes of dreams."

—Miles Harvey, *The Island of Lost Maps*

Tabula universalis Orbis Ptolemaeo cogniti, based on Ptolemy's (100–170) cosmology, dates to 1420

I.

The Ancient and Medieval World

Lascaux Cave Paintings of Stars

This is a mystical place
encouraging us to look
up and compare what we see with
what our Paleolithic ancestors
saw and depicted on their cave walls.
Was it an event that took place
in a dream or a shaman's vision,
yet very real?

Ptolemy's *Geographia*

Ptolemy's World Map, c. 150
"I know that I am mortal by nature, and ephemeral;
but when I trace my pleasure the windings to and
fro of the heavenly bodies I no longer touch the
earth with my feet: I stand in the presence of Zeus
himself and take my fill of ambrosia."

—*Almagest*, Ptolemy, 100–170 CE

My work enabled astronomers to make
accurate predictions of planetary positions
and solar and lunar eclipses.
Centuries will pass as scientists
in many fields consider my work.
But no one will know that my love
for music and poetry was not theoretical.
I wrote poetry, forever lost, about passion,
the ephemeral, the fragility of life, the stunning
beauty of the stars, never to be captured
by astronomical study.

Water Is the Driving Force of All Nature

*"When once you have tasted flight, you will forever walk the
earth with your eyes turned skyward, for there you have been,
and there you will always long to return."*
                    —attributed to Leonardo da Vinci, 1452–1519

Where do the freed birds go at night,
after I release them from their cages?
I, Leonardo di ser Piero da Vinci
wish no harm to any animal.
I do not eat them or want them
to be in captivity. I imagine
their freedom in flight, and sometimes
think to map it, but that is a betrayal
of their sovereignty to soar through
the skies as they please, as far as they may.
They now belong to no one
but their feathered comrades.

I will not paint today,
but will work on drawing
a map of a watershed, just begun—
a bird's eye view of part of Tuscany.
When this task is complete
I will have drawn three
topographic maps of Tuscany.

I have recognized that water flows
over and under the surface of Earth
in a pattern, not unlike human veins.
I will use washes of different intensities
to follow the contours of mountain
chains, different shades representing
different elevations, and will picture
the rivers, valleys, and settlements
in a realistic manner.

My fascination with landscapes
can be recognized in several
of my celebrated paintings.
Many have noticed with curiosity
and intrigue the winding road,
the bridge, the lakes and mountains
behind the *Mona Lisa*.

If I am remembered for nothing else,
I have repeatedly recognized in all

of my work that water is the driving
force of all nature.

Ultimately, it must be understood
that in rivers, for a prime example,
the water you touch is the last
of what has passed and the first

of that which comes.
So with present time.

Galileo's Cartography and Dante's Cosmology

Infernal cosmology and calculating the dimensions of Hell

I doubt that in centuries to come
I will not be well-known for
my map of hell, but rather
for my confirmation of the theory
of the heliocentric universe
judged by the church
as heresy and condemning me
to prison and, later, house arrest,
for the remainder of my life.
But I know what I knew—
that the sun was the center
of the universe

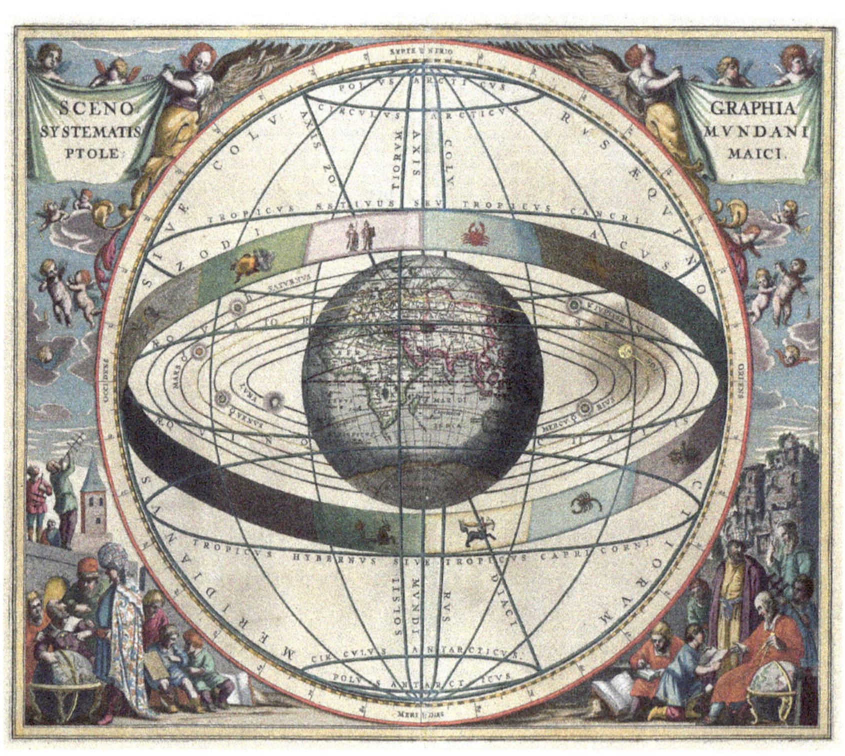

Andreas Cellarius (1596–1665), *Scenographia Systematis Mundani Ptolemaici,* a celestial chart that illustrates the geocentric (Earth-centered) model of the universe as theorized by Ptolemy

II.

"There is a great deal of unmapped country within us which would have to be taken into account as an explanation of our gusts and storms."
—George Eliot, *Daniel Deronda*

Drafting My Desire

Love is my cartographer—
I draw lines from your hand
to your right shoulder,
from your left shoulder
to your right hand where
I trace the lines of your palm
noting shallow rivers,
tributaries, and perpendicular
routes to your destiny.

I follow the path
of your sternum, imagine
the shape of your heart,
drafting my desire, hoping
to formulate the meaning
of desire as a terrain
even more dangerous,
even more mysterious
than love.

Naked

Cartography of a tryst

We hike the Stevens Gulch Trail
on a summer afternoon, climbing past
tree line, beyond the tundra, until
we reach scoured gray rocks, ringing
the last oval of crystalline snow.
The wind starts up and we walk down
a ways, stopping between patches
of tundra, until we reach coarse grass.

Our dog sniffs the air
and paces around us.
He wants to run, and seems
disappointed that we just sit,
staring down into the valley
where everything is far away:
tiny pine trees for a dollhouse
world and the creek a slender stream
of silver, winding east. We lie
on our backs, watching clouds
flowing past the sun.

The dog lies beside us, head on his paws,
whining softly, wanting to be on his way
down the trail, running among the trees.
I unzip my shorts, slide them past
my ankles and off. You watch me,
running your hand down my thigh
and calf before unbuttoning your shirt.

When we are naked on the bare mountain,
we face each other until we are seamless,
breastbones to toes, breathing together
in time, out of time.

His Map

Before he left he drew
me a map with his fine
set of colored pencils.
"Don't leave," he said,
"until after the Vernal
Equinox, when the days
have grown even longer
and the first flowers
have sprung to life.
Follow the map
and we'll be together soon."
"I'm afraid," I said. "Why
can't I travel with you?"
"I am preparing the cottage
for you, for your comfort.
You may encounter magic
along the way, but nothing
sinister, no ghosts."

I saw the woods emerging,
penciled green on either
side of the path that gained
altitude, then leveled off.

"Take care, for someday
after we are both gone
the map will be found
in a museum or gallery."

After he left, I packed
a rucksack and set off.
I saw the woods emerging
true to how they had been
drawn, but alive and deep
in shadows, filled with birds.

I ventured off the path
drawn on the map.
Off the path, butterflies
formed a canopy, and the dust
from their wings glittered
as it floated down.
I am covered in silken air.
Though I won't return
to the path, I am not
far from my destination.
Will the moon come back?
I want to hear birdsongs.
I step further into the forest.
I hear the river I must reach
to explain river, to
explain water.
Clutching the map, I
understand the difference
between his map
and my desire.

Public Discourse

Map the contemporary universe
of discourse by determining
the magical, authoritarian, and
ritual elements of language.

Magical language is symbolic
terrain that must be mapped,
now uncharted, but chartable.

Evoke some magic words.
Cast a spell. Declare your soul name.

The connection between humans
and the world is always
mediated by the word.

Authoritarian language is the terrain
of power: Obey the rules.
Do what you are told.
Describe the kind of tyrant
you are and will always be.

Ritual language is the terrain
of the profane and the sacred.

Curse and pray, employ incantation.
Consecrate language as a suburb
or ancient city: map it; synoptically
represent the words you blurt
and locate them in space.

I Map My Life's Tattoo

I map my internal terrain,
my brain, particularly the pre-frontal
cortex, where I explore my will
to live, and moderate my erratic
behavior, changing with storms,
full moons, and indecision.
My heart beats. Where is it
lodged? Forget the emotional
terrain of the heart that is too
difficult to map and solely
consider its placement in
the body as you locate it
by its beating, beating, beating.

I then map my external terrain,
feet on the earth, moving
toward a destination
for me to follow, and as I
walk forward I observe patterns
and watch tree limbs sway
in a light wind as I map
my life's tattoo. What
is my destination, measured
by directions, a way lost
here and a way lost there?

I measure and compute,
understanding that I have
mapped my way and I
am not lost, but a mere
traveler in psychic
time and corporeal space.
I am my own cartographer.

Crown Hill Cemetery

GPS Coordinates:
Latitude 39.75810, Longitude -105.09420

Before I go, I print a map
to help me wend my way
from monuments, to gated
vaults, to simple stones, to
brass plaques set flush to grass.

I stop, too often, to read
dates of birth and death
and other messages.

I turn right on a path
and soon I am standing
in the Garden of Reflection.
What will happen if I
become lost in reflection?
What kind of map will show
me the way out of unceasing
reflection—its alluring wonderment.

So I walk out of this garden
and continue down the path.
I can vanish in here,
Among the vaults and stones,
the wilting flowers.
I read, "Just whisper my name
and I will be there."

"The wind that gave me my first
breath also received my last sigh."
Damien Parlor, August 1, 1974–
September 27, 1984, "Child of light,

bridge in the universe. A boy
who could pet bees." Now I
am in a section of the cemetery
dedicated to children.

I walk through Memory Meadow,
Further into the quadrant of earth
designated "Child's Place" where
shrubs and flowers border the stretch
of green, well-tended grass.
Atop a two-tiered circle of stones
stand two marble figures—a lamb
and a small boy. The boy stoops,
seeming to look into the lamb's eyes.

A woman rests her head on a marble
marker and weeps, wrenching cries.
Here the earth overflows with tears.

I Am Lost

I had a map, beautiful
and ornate as an early
Roman stone map, hand-
colored as an eighteenth-
century scientific projection.
It was a singular, valuable map
that must have slipped
from my backpack.

Foolishly, I retraced my
steps, not knowing, without
my map, if I was heading
in the right direction.
You may rightfully ask
where I was going.
Without my map I can't
answer the question.

Was it to a mythological
place turned into
reality by my map?

Now having no shadow
but myself, I wait urgently
for darkness and the ephemeral
light of the stars.

Matthäus Seutter (1678–1757), *Tabula Anemographica seu Pyxis Nautica,* a Baroque-style wind chart featuring decorative wind heads surrounding compass roses and allegorical images of the seasons

III.

Consider. Is existence a miracle? And if so, can
"Maps codify the miracle of existence"?
—Nicholas Cane, *Mercator: The Man
Who Mapped the Planet*

Who Am I?

Galaxies, like many things we map
do not have precise boundaries.
Yet what is a boundary but
an imaginary line, dusty
as a shadow?

Who am I to map the Milky Way,
non-scientist, puny human,
but I view the constellation Sagittarius,
my sign, so I will take some ownership,
and also, it is Thursday, reputedly my lucky day.
Big numbers: 13 billion years
old, 400 billion stars,
with a black hole at the center, which, along with
the rest of the universe is moving through space.

Who am I to map the Milky Way?
What might our galaxy look like from
an interstellar spaceship including
the distances and positions of more
than eight thousand bright stars, star
clusters, and giant molecular clouds?

Described by the ancients as a river, as milk,
and as a path, among other things, the band
has been visible in the heavens since
Earth first formed.

In daylight, I look up, imagining what is above
me, seeing only a veil of transparent cirrostratus
clouds, fibrous, nearly covering the whole sky.

At night, I look up. No moon shines, yet.
Since I live in the city, few stars or constellations
or planets reveal themselves. I think of
the images of astro-photographers who have
captured the spiral galaxy: reflected in a pool,
the green airglow, the Magellanic Cloud,
Jupiter at the center, and to its left, Antares.

I map the universe, with the surety that I love,
make love, and seek love.

Mapping the Ephemeral

Stratus

Stratus are flat, hazy, featureless clouds,
low altitude, varying in color from
dark gray to nearly white.
"Featureless." We can then
see rabbits or giraffes, or even
the face of a former lover.

Stratus is a huge blanket
often covering the entire sky.
When white, the water droplets
reflect all of the colors of light.
So if white, they contain
a hidden spectrum of beauty.
When dark, light cannot
penetrate, and they are low
to the ground, and we see
them as fog or mist, reminding
us of dreams, where we apprehend
things clearly, even through
the mist of the past, of memory.

Stratocumulus

Stratocumulus clouds extensively
layer the sky in sheets of grey
or low white clouds that cover
the sky, but sometimes you
can see patches of blue through
the cloud field. Sometimes the patches
merge, tantalizingly, mesmerizingly.

It's easy to imagine that behind
those clouds something more
than the blue is hidden. Some mysteries
are easier to bear than others. Some
are not. This is not toying with metaphysics,
but the realities of mysteries observed
in the natural world.

Cumulus

Six-year-old, hunched over creamy paper
outlining in number 2 pencil and no shading.
To her, this is the cloud that symbolizes
all clouds, every cloud she will see for years,
brilliant white when the sun shines through.
She wishes she could sketch the sun's light,
but all she manages is to create a puffy shape.
Now, it's a bunny, on paper, but
when she looks into the sky
again, it has morphed into
a turtle with a shiny white dome.
Fair weather, today.

Bombed-out Cities

Wars now, TEN TO WATCH: Syria/ISIS
Ukraine S.Sudan Nigeria Congo Afghanistan

Cartographies of Bombed Out Cities in Syria

I walk upon an earth that has no map.
Aleppo
I walk through the streets of Aleppo,
one of the oldest inhabited cities in the world.
It has been all but obliterated by barrel bombs,
bullets, chemical attacks and air strikes in the war.
No street signs remain, so I walk, following a tank,
among the photographers who refuse to leave.

Where do boys keep their toy soldiers,
plastic replicas of flesh and blood infantry?
Guns and tanks spilled onto a living room
rug that swirls with blood-colored flowers.

Class-Five Hurricane

I.

I sit with my eyes glued to the television.
Is there a less clichéd way to describe an
obsession with wild, unpredictable weather?
I've been through hurricanes, tornadoes,
pounding thunderstorms, thunder, lightning.
The adrenaline thrill is shameful. Waiting
for the Eye. Everything to lose.

The radar visuals are stunning: Ever
changing swirls of brilliant color.
Fire red, bordering a blaze of orange,
blue and green and yellow.
No artist's renderings, these
visuals are the real thing.

The Copernicus Sentinel
satellite tells the truth of the storm's
devastating, whirling trajectory.
"Spaghetti model" is a delicious-
sounding term that has nothing
to do with food, but rather strands
showing the "where" and "when"
of tropical storms and hurricanes.

I watch the surges, the flooded streets,
brown people, poor people, people holding
children in arms, trudging through
waist-high water, houses flattened to rubble.

II.

Now this: Looters with machetes,
head-on collisions, family animals
chained to trees, prisoners left behind.
No water, no electricity a POTUS
who's never heard of a class-five
hurricane but says there were worse
hurricanes in the 30s and 40s . . . and,
this time: "38 deaths. Unfortunate they
passed, but such a small number. Not bad."
Oh yeah, say that to their families.
Not bad.
Recycle and everything will be okay?
Take the bus, turn out the lights, buy
a hybrid and everything will be okay?
No matter what the deniers say, this
is a new world . . . one we are not ready for.

Sleepers

I.

The long-married couple
sleep in their Temper pedic bed,
adjusted for him and for her.
They wear identical button-to-
the-neck gray pajamas.
Their sleepwear is unadorned
by polka dots or stars or
colorful animals, so what
do they dream of? Empty rooms
or other worlds or moonscapes?
When they arise, they don't
tell their dream stories.

II.

Animals have made
impressions in the tall grass.
Their shapes are retained:
coyote, fox, small dog, big
dog, feral cats, a fawn.
They lie head to tail,
peaceably, in comfort.
They neither growl,
claw, nor bite.
At dawn they awaken
and go their separate
ways until dusk when
they curl together again
for warmth and dreamless sleep.

III.

"Don't sit or lie on the grates,"
  read signs everywhere.
  So, fearing arrest, they are left
  to dark corners, lying in worn
  sleeping bags or covered
  by thin blankets.
  They are anathemas
  to the city officials who want
  to hide them, denying their
  needs, their suffering.
"They are responsible."
"They need to find jobs."
"They use panhandling money
  to buy drugs or liquor."
"They fight." "They swear."
  If they sleep at all, their
  sleep is fitful. They thrash
  and turn. When they do sleep
  they cry out in unintelligible syllables.

In these sounds are heard both
their nightmares and their dreams.

The Light-Spangled City,
the Distant Railroad Tracks

We walked for miles
from Penn Station
to reach our Airbnb,
ending up at 127th St.
just north of Central Park.

It was dark by the time we
rode the elevator to the 18th
floor and looked out over
the city and the distant railroad tracks.

We drank wine, then, before
we set out again, more walking,
past liquor stores, small markets,
and more—hole-in-the-wall
apartments, barber shops, nail
salons, and black men
and a few women sitting on
benches, talking, smoking,
drawing on their 40s
or sipping from plastic flasks.

My husband struck up
a conversation with a group.
"What do you think now
that Trump's been elected president?"
The chorus of voices came on strong.
"He ain't my president!!"
"He won't do nothin' for us.
"Don't you think no different
or you a fool."
"We're gonna live here
and we're gonna die here
on the streets of South Harlem."

Meditation

I.   Meditate

Lay down a cushion, attempt
the Lotus position, and do
not allow yourself to feel pain.
Remember . . . no, that's wrong . . .
for you must clear your mind
of all but the present moment.
Last night I dreamed . . . no.
Be here now, you say, thinking
you must rest in the emptiness of mind.
What obstacles will I face?

How do I stop thinking?
What is the goal?
To end suffering? And what
is suffering? Are you asking
for a kind of grace to end it?
The bell rings. Sit quite straight.
Close your eyes. Nothing comes
from outside the mind.
is it time to stand up?
Has the bell rung yet?

II. A Map of the Brain during Meditation

"Someone *is* breathing inside me—
    birds, the very earth."

Can meditation change the mind?
Meditation generates gamma waves,
indicating that a meditating brain
is doing something, perhaps
generating feelings of loving kindness.

After long hours of mental training
high levels of brain activity
can be mapped in the meditator.
Is it really possible, as Gandhi
famously advised, to be the change
we seek in the world by careful
breathing and calming our minds?
Listen to the sound inside yourself.
An echo. *Om shrim.* Peace . . . peace.

Cartography of the Seasons

I.   Winter

My mind is amorphous,
refusing, like a cloud,
to retain its form.
My mind is a rabbit hopping
from one plant to another,
stretching languidly until
it is a white snake refusing
to stay still, to be caught.
That is the winter mind,
informed by cold, crystal
pinpoints in the frigid air.

II. *Spring*

The spring mind, like
spring itself, grows
and sometimes flowers,
scenting the air.
Clusters of flowers
inhabit my mind.
My mind is amorphous,
yet resilient at the same time:
resilient to contradiction,
to contradictory impulses.

If you could hold my mind
like a clump of fresh-
turned earth and bring it
close to your nose,
it would have a distinct
aroma, but not at all
like those first clusters
of flowers. The scent
of my spring mind is of
warmth, surprise,
of overturned darkness.

III.   Summer

Heat radiates through
the summer mind.
The summer mind eyes
clouds, abundant
cumulus clouds
with shimmering contours.
Ah, the summer mind
expands with sunlight
and warm, brisk wind.
The summer mind knows
the preciousness of long
languid days and the burgeoning
garden, colors exquisite
at high noon: shining
purple eggplant, jalapeno
peppers and serranos and
Thai peppers unstoppable
fill the summer mind
with a gaudy, explosive collage.
The summer mind must be
cautious, protective, remembering
that "ripeness is all," and
that over-ripeness is never
a gift.

IV.   Autumn

Oh, the mind says, your
love of October light
is a cliché. Don't you
know that? You want
to talk back to the know-
it-all autumn mind.
Its exactitude and pomposity
can be hurtful. Yet,
the summer mind can
take you through the rows
of still-abundant—
for just a while longer—
strawberries and raspberries,
treating your explorations
with attentive kindness.
The autumn mind tries
to prepare you for tendrils
of frost and snowy roads, and
for the time that "seasons
of mists and mellow
fruitfulness" will be over.

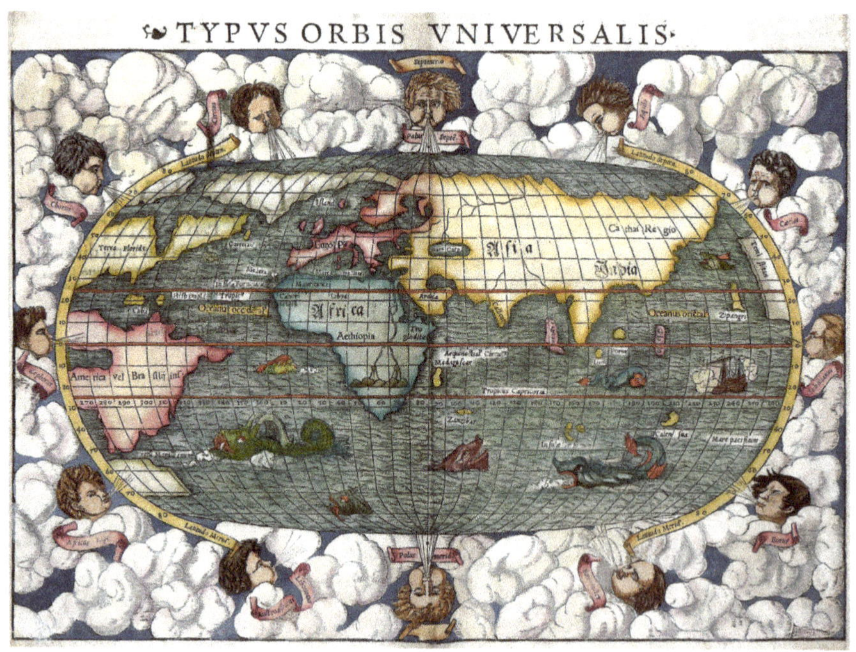

Sebastian Muenster, (1488–1552), *Typus Orbis Universalis*, based on Ptolemy's (100–170) cosmology

IV.

"A map does not just chart, it unlocks
and formulates meaning."
—Reif Larsen

Mapping Middle Earth

I was offended when C. S.
Lewis said I could not "draw
lions." Of course not, though
I could draw animals, many kinds
for many children's books, including
the books of Tolkien. I have
always been especially fond
of drawing dogs, who have
been my constant companions,
but I am a mapmaker, a cartographer,
though should my name be put
forward in a trivia quiz, no
one could identify me, Pauline
Baynes, acclaimed illustrator.

My interest in world religion
and cultures made me
uncomfortable with the narrowly
Christian allegory of the Narnia
stories, but nevertheless,
I mapped the places that
emerged from Tolkien's text,
and he, in turn praised my work.
When, later, I shared my artwork
for a poster featuring Frodo and Bilbo
Baggins, Tolkien nodded approvingly
and half-whispered, "There
they are. There they are."

I played Haydn in intervals
as I worked, being especially
fond of his Sonata in E minor.
Of himself Haydn said,
"I never was a quick writer,
but composed with great
care and effort." His words

and his music helped
me formulate my
identity as an artist

I had a stillborn daughter.
Only one of my biographers
reported that Fritz and I never
had children and another said
we chose not to have children.
Untrue. She was perfectly
formed and I called her
"Clair de Lune," knowing
she would ever be to me
most ghostly, most exquisite
moonlight. Fritz and I
scattered her ashes
in the beautiful garden
my studio overlooked,
where my ashes would

also be scattered.
Dear Claire, if I could
have drawn a map
you could have followed
into the living world,
I would have done so,
but that was beyond
my frail powers. I
was a cartographer who
knew precision and detail,
but not magic.

Literary Maps

Is the map the territory
or is it not? Is it an
abstraction taken to
be the real thing?
What is the utility
of a 1:1 map as
Lewis Carroll affirmed
in *Sylvie and Bruno
Concluded?*

"And then came the grandest
idea of all! We actually made
a map of the country, on the scale
of a mile to the mile!"
1:1 maps are absurd, using
the country itself as its own map.

Not only is the map not the territory,
but the territory can't be folded
up and put in your pocket.

William Faulkner begged to differ.
In a *Paris Review* interview he said,
to describe his hand-drawn map
of Yoknapatawpha County,
"I created a cosmos of my own."
He signed the map, "WILLIAM
FAULKNER, SOLE OWNER
AND PROPRIETOR," leaving
no doubt that he believed the map
he drew made him sole owner
of the territory that he conceived
of as mythical soil, and of
the Yoknapatawpha map,

claiming knowledge as power;
map as territory.

Three Sisters

I.

Last week a woman from Boston
walking along the beach was picked
off by a rogue and taken to sea.
She wasn't found until the next day.
Awful to think of the cartography
of her journey. Could anyone
have mapped her trip from
sea to shore? Freak waves,
monster waves, killer
waves, sneaker waves.
Never turn your back
on the ocean.
Freak waves are the stuff
of legend. They
always appear from
nowhere, and disappear
without a trace.

II.

On Lake Superior,
a group of three rogue waves,
called "three sisters,"
is suspected as one of the causes
for the sinking of the Fitzgerald
on November 10, 1975.
Twenty-nine crew members were lost.
Because these waves follow each other
closely, ships can't recover and shed
the water from the first wave before the others
strike, which leads to sinkings.
The captain of a ship near
the Fitzgerald reported that his ship
was hit by two 30- to 35-foot waves.
These waves, followed by a third, continued
in the direction of the Fitzgerald and may
have struck about the same time it sank.

Ocean and lake rogue waves are rare
and can strike with tremendous force.
A thirty-nine foot wave has a breaking
force of six metric tons per square meter
[t/m2] (8.5 psi).
"The Wreck of the *Edmund Fitzgerald*"
by Gordon Lightfoot,
a song that only adds to the legend of this ship.
The *Edmund Fitzgerald* was the largest ship
ever to sink in Lake Superior

Delicate Indeed. Yet So Fragile

Elizabeth Bishop talks about her poem "The Map"

I was very ill with asthma and the flu, and was alone
on New Year's Eve in my tiny Greenwich Village
flat, an unadorned place where that bleak evening

I began to stare at a map, a framed map of the North
Atlantic, containing the Maritime Provinces,
Greenland, Iceland, and Scandinavia.

I was sitting on the floor, imagining travel
and appreciating the mapmaker's colors
that I incorporated in my poem: "shadowed
green," "the fine tan sandy shelf,"

"Labrador's yellow." I ask, "can the countries
pick their colors?" And again I ask, "What
suits the character or the native waters best?"

Is this not a crucial question about maps?
Poetry, like cartography, can condense
the world aesthetically, until we see
that the last line of my poem is not ambiguous,
but lucid, perfectly lucid: "More delicate than
the historians' are the map-makers' colors."

Delicate, indeed. So fine in texture,
yet so fragile.

In Time. Out of Time

A calendar is a map of time,
but a calendar is an abstraction.
What do we know of calendars
written in the ancient world?
Are they based on legends?
The traces that survive might
be dates inscribed on tombstones
or written on parchment.

When classical writers quote
earlier authorities and their
view on maps, it might be
the case that some of their
claims are based on the game
known as "telephone," where
the transmitted stories of maps
become increasingly inaccurate.
Aristotle, for example, is renowned
for repeating far-fetched travelers' tales.

A personal time-map is a mirror.
Color-code your calendar with
the hourly activities of your day,
and shade the area to indicate
how well you think you
performed each task.
Daily, you will see
a cornucopia of color.
Blue for an hour of writing,
only lightly shaded, and green
for exercise, many miles,
well shaded; choose your
palette as you regard this
mapping of your calendar
not as a compulsion, but as
a means of becoming mindful.

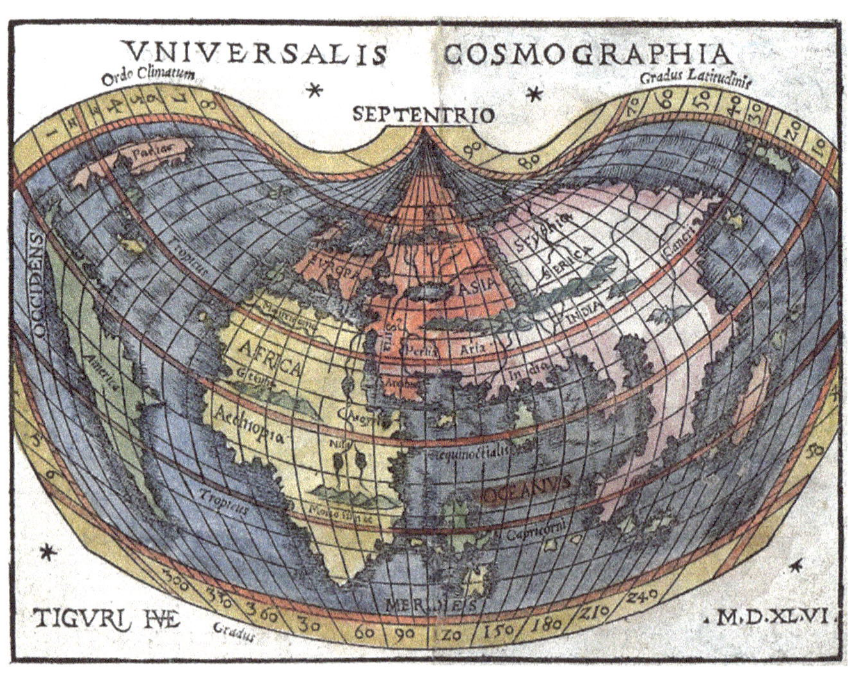

Johannes Honter (1498–1549), *Universalis Cosmographia,* a heart-shaped (cordiform) world map known for its depiction of the northern coast of Asia connecting to the North Pole and the use of the term "America"

V.

"A map says to you, 'Read me carefully, follow
me closely, doubt me not.' It says, 'I am the earth
in the palm of your hand. Without me,
you are alone and lost.'"
—Beryl Markham, *West with the Wind*

The Ascent of Nanga Parbat

Situated: Punjab Himalaya
Longitude: 74 degrees 35' 24" E
Latitude: 35 degrees 14" 21" N

[The] Name is derived from Sanskrit *Nanga Parvata* meaning "Naked Mountain." In Dardi, as legend will have it, the name means "Dwelling place of the fairies," who supposedly live near the summit.

Louis C. Baume, *Sivilaya: Explorations of the 8000-metre Peaks of the Himalaya*

Killer Mountain has earned its morbid nickname.
More than 30 climbers died on Nanga Parbat
before it was eventually summited in 1953,
according to the BBC.

Base camp in Fairy Meadows.
Day01: Islamabad - Chilas
Day02: Chilas - Fairy Meadows
Day03: Trek to Byal camp and Nanga Parbat Base camp
Day04: Fairy Meadows - Chilas
Day05: Chilas - Islamabad

1953: Austro-German expedition
First Successful Ascent

Our ten-member party arrived
at Gilgit, Pakistan, by air.
The route continued to the Indus
River, and we followed it down
to the Rakhiot Bridge and turned south
past Fairy Meadows—where
there are 400 species of flowers.
We set up a base camp on the site
of earlier expeditions.

I, Hermann Buhl, a member of a German-Austrian
team, climbed, via the Rakhiot Flank (East Ridge),
on July 3. I continued up the Silver Plateau.
My final push for the summit was dramatic.
I continued alone for the final 1300 meters,
after my companions had turned back.
I was under the influence of the drugs pervitin
and tea from coca leaves. I reached the summit
40 hours later, dangerously late, at 7 p.m.,
the climbing harder and more time-consuming
than I had anticipated. I decided not
to return along the North Ridge,
but to descend by the snow face
down to Diamair Gap. My descent
was slowed when I lost a crampon.

Caught by darkness, I was forced
to bivouac standing upright on a narrow
ledge, grasping a small handhold with one hand.
Exhausted, I dozed occasionally, but managed
to maintain my balance. I was also fortunate
to have a calm night, so I was not subjected
to wind chill. I finally reached my high camp
at 7 p.m. the next day, 40 hours after setting out.

I made the ascent without oxygen.
I am the only man to have made the first
ascent of an 8000 m peak alone.

Geography: An Illusion

Johannes Vermeer, *The Geographer*

I am Vermeer's creation
in an imagined room filled with
maps, charts, a globe, and books
rendered on canvas.
At first Vermeer had me looking
down rather than looking out
a window, where in a final
version of the painting I
squint in the sunlight seeming
to think intently, ready
to experience a revelation.

The dividers I hold
were originally vertical,
not horizontal.

The cartographic objects
in his painting suggest
his familiarity with
the profession that obsessed
the Netherlands in the 17th
Century.

Half obscured, the sea chart
on a wall behind me depicts
all of the sea coasts
of Europe.

Who am I? What did
I know of perspective?
Reputedly, I Anthonie
van Leeuwhoek posed not
once, but twice for Vermeer.

But I was an expert in microscopy,
not peeping idly out a window,
as if the landscape I saw was actual.
My landscape of *animalcules*—
tiny animals—seen under
my lens—is my life's geography.
No illusionary place, but *prima
materia*, where all I see has come
to be real. Has come to be wondrous.

Marie Tharp's Cartography of the Ocean Floor

Girl Talk

My maps proved Continental Drift—plate tectonics—was real.
I discovered the 10,000-mile-long Mid-Atlantic Ridge—
also called "the backbone of earth," a series of mountainous
ridges deep below the surface of the ocean. And if you've ever
seen a map of our planet, you've seen my work.

I alone, translated nearly indecipherable columns
of numbers recorded from 1940s-era ocean
research expeditions—that I was not allowed
to join, being a woman and considered "bad luck"—
into detailed, hand-drawn maps of the world's oceans.

I found inspiration in the very mystery of the task.
The whole world was spread out before me.
I had a blank canvas to fill.

Studying the crack in the ocean floor, I could see
it was too large, too contiguous, to be anything
but a rift valley, a place where two masses
of land had separated. When I compared it
to a rift valley in Africa, I grew more certain.
But when I showed Bruce Heezen, my research
supervisor (four years my junior), "he groaned
and said, 'It can't be. It looks too much
like continental drift." I wrote later:
"Bruce initially dismissed my interpretation
of the profiles as 'girl talk.'" With the lab's
reputation on the line, Heezen ordered me
to redo the map. I went back to the data
and started plotting again from scratch.

In 1959 Bruce and I completed our first
map of the North Atlantic. After Bruce died in 1977
I focused my energy on completing a comprehensive
view of the world's oceans, illuminating a hidden
world of rifts and valleys, volcanic ranges stretching
for thousands of miles and mountain peaks taller than Everest.

I loved, like Marie Curie, to work in my
garden, but had little time. I quote her:
"I am held to my work by a thousand bonds."

Paper Towns, Trap Streets

Where is Agloe, New York?

Agloe is a fake town that became real, and for
a time really existed. And then it didn't.
It's been said that Agloe's story might be
the strangest in the already strange
history of copyright traps in maps.

Otto G. Lindberg of General Drafting
Company and his assistant Ernest Alpers
invented Agloe, mixing their initials: OGL and EA.
If a competitor happened to have the same
fake town on his map, they knew they
had caught a plagiarist. But then they
saw it on a Rand McNally map.
Lindberg insisted Agloe did not
exist, but then it did. It wasn't real,
then it became real, when suddenly
there was an "Agloe General Store."

"I traveled there," writes a well-known
journalist. After veering off Exit 94
for Roscoe and heading a few miles
north, there it was: Nestled below
the Catskill Mountains on a windy
two-lane road, there was a tall
green sign that read: "Welcome
to Agloe! Home of the Agloe
General Store. Come back soon!"

There are fake towns, there are real
towns, and then there is Agloe
in upstate New York. The town
was invented as a cartographical
ploy in the 1930s, but it somehow
ended up becoming real. Agloe's

story might be the strangest
in the already strange history
of copyright traps in maps.

Usually, mapmakers don't invent
whole towns out of paper and ink.
Usually, they craft more subtle traps:
nonexistent dead ends or fake river
bends or adjusted mountain elevations.
Mapmakers rarely officially admit
to "trap streets," but it's an age-old
practice to keep copycats at bay.
Yet there are trees, the sharp sun
of fall, a barking dog,
the murmuring of birds,
as in any town.
But it is easier here
to identify with ghosts.

Dark Matter

"Why does dark matter have to be witnessed by anyone?"
—Levi Bryant

The movement of stars and galaxies
indicates that the Universe is also made
up of invisible particles called dark matter.
The highest-resolution maps of dark
matter offer a detailed case
for the existence of cold dark matter—
sluggish particles comprising
the bulk of matter in the universe.
Cold dark matter moves slowly
compared to the speed of light,
while hot dark matter moves faster.

The granularity of dark matter has supposedly
been mapped in exquisite detail, and the most
detailed topographical map of the dark
matter landscape has been produced.

Questions remain: How far
can we go in understanding
what we have never really seen?
Does dark matter border
on cosmological mysticism?
And therefore despite Hubble
images, can dark matter be mapped?

Dark matter is the stuff
that both is and is not.
What leads to scientific truth?
Is it purely physical reality?

The Infectious Well

I am John Snow, a Soho doctor.
I have studied and calculated
dosages for the use of ether and
chloroform as surgical anesthetics,
allowing my patients to undergo
surgical procedures with much
diminished distress and pain.

I administered chloroform
to Queen Victoria when she
gave birth to her eighth
child, Prince Leopold.

I have long been a skeptic
of miasma theory that claims
diseases such as cholera
and bubonic plague are
caused by bad air.

The cholera epidemic in 1854
led me to trace the source
of the spread of disease by
mapping every case of cholera
from this plague.

I have called it the "most
terrible outbreak of cholera
that ever occurred in this kingdom."
A woman who lived at 40 Broad Street,
whose child who had contracted
cholera from some other source,
washed the baby's diapers in water
she then dumped into a leaky cesspool
just three feet from the Broad Street pump.

By using a geographical grid to map
deaths from the outbreak and investigating
each case to determine access
to the pump water, I developed
positive proof the pump
was the source of the epidemic.
I was not a hero, but a simple
physician determined to establish
that waters polluted by bacteria
are the source of this disease.

People Get Ready

Martin Luther King called Curtis Mayfield's
song one of the most important lyrics
of the Civil Rights Movement.

I am nameless. You don't need to know my name
There are thousands like me. What desperation
has led me to leave the plantation, knowing
I would be put to death if I did not succeed in my flight?
Already, I have walked in the woods for days.
Hungry, cold, hidden in a box or under a load of hay.
Soon I hope to meet my first conductor who
will direct me to the next station shepherding
me to freedom in the North, where

I will no longer be anyone's slave.
From Owego to Danby I am directed to follow
a route that will take me to the AME Zion
Church in Ithaca, a terminal where I will
rest until I continue north, getting closer
to Canada as I walk and perhaps meet
another fugitive, a fellow as terrified
as I am.

I am nameless.
You don't need to know
my name. There are thousands like me
who will never again hear the whip crack
or feel it burn into flesh.

Bashō's Narrow Road to the Interior

Every day is a journey, and the journey itself is home.
    —Bashō, 1689

First I will devise a mental map, then
a spiritual map, and finally a physical map.
I know that the three routes
will often intertwine as they
should in a long journey.

I will set out in late spring
with my companion Kawai Sora
My pack will be made heavier
with farewell gifts from friends.

I leave behind my friends but
cannot leave without their gifts.
Travel these days is very
dangerous, but I am
committed to wandering,
and before departing,

I prepare my mind for a long
journey to far provinces.
I will sell my house
and dress as a monk,
"to feel the truth
of the old poems."
I will visit places
made famous by poems.

To begin the journey
we take a boat from Edo
and reach the docks of Senju.
Then we leave on foot to begin
our journey to Matsu and Dewa.

Our travel makes us age,
meaning seeing the world
is daily making us wiser.
We reach a post station at Soka.
Sora and I eventually reach
Muro-no-yashima,a shrine,
honoring "Ko-no-hana-sakuya-hime",
a goddess worshiped at the base of Mount Fuji.
Later, we lodge at an inn in the Nikko Mountains.
A month later, Sora and I leave to worship
at another shrine at the Nikko Mountains.

I am asked, "is this your *jisei?*
your death poem?"

Sick on my journey,
only my dreams will wander
these desolate moors.

Tabi ni yande
yume wa kareno wo
kakemeguru

"There is no verse in my life
which is not a farewell poem.
So if someone asks for my
farewell poem, any verse
I composed of recent years
may be my farewell one:

The old pond
a frog jumping in
the sound of water

Furu ike ya
kawasu tobikomu
misu no oto

A flower, like human life,
grows, blooms, withers,
and is finally blown away.

What Happens When Dream Logic Shatters?

This poem is a map
about other maps both
physical and metaphysical.
You may own, or have
at least seen, a Rand McNally
Road Atlas, first printed in 1924.
In the Atlas, we can browse
maps of physical places throughout.
The map's legend is a place to start:

Roads are ribbons of color, green,
blue, red, and grey, and dotted lines
for roads under construction, helping
us to imagine physical terrains.

If you've ever been to Florida
and have been lucky enough
to visit the Everglades you'll see
on the map, the edge of mangroves
stitched by a red line.
The mangroves are swatches
of dark green, from Pavilion
Key to the north and East
Cape to the south.

The string of Keys is darker
green, seeming to float in the blue-
blue Gulf of Mexico to the north
and the Atlantic to the south.
Tangible. Key West lies
about one degree from
the Tropic of Cancer
(23 1/2 degrees N. Lat.),
which marks the beginning of the Tropics.
Physical. An easy-to-follow map,
until the water rises or a

hurricane alters the shoreline.
Metaphysical maps offer
us guidance through worlds
that are different from
physical worlds.
Are metaphysical maps
more or less reliable
than physical maps?
Physical maps help us
move through material worlds.

All maps are metaphysical
in that they depict things
beyond accuracy, not just
telling us how to get somewhere,
but passing judgment on reality
when they tell us where we are.

Consider the Map of Prana:
Showing the full spectrum
of energy…human figure
receiving direct cosmic
energy to the head, sunlight
to the face, energy generated
externally from the chest
through the knees; electro-
magnetism coming from the earth.

And in the
dream map: where
and who are the dream's personae?
What emotions can the dreamer
perceive and how do characters
in the dream behave?

Who are they?
Who is the dreamer?

Does the dreamer
live inside the dream,
waiting for what happens
when dream logic
shatters?

How Maps Become Real

Maps become real
as one reads.

Utopia
Royaume d'Amour
Lilliput
Avalon
The Land of Oz

Mapping involves
interpretation
and re-interpretation
is always subjective.

Middle Earth
Earthsea
Macondo
Treasure Island
Narnia

Maps of imaginary
worlds comment
on the relationship
between seeing
and knowing.

What do we wish
we knew?

What do we think
we know?

Huckleberry Finn's Mississippi Journey
Yowknapatopha County
The Princess Bride
Walden Pond

Game of Thrones
Gotham City
Never Neverland
And many more . . .

*The map may be
saying to the reader*

*"You are here,
 you are really here."*

Festival at Ship Rock

Some years ago, I was a counselor
at the St. Francis Center, a Day
Center, a safe place, a resource
geared to the homeless population.
Today, I am a manager there whose
thoughts are a chaos of dreams
and memories and…maps.
Maps that lie yellowing
in a seldom-visited drawer.

I became friends with many
clients at the Center, but
Nelson Begay struck a chord—
a sometimes dissonant chord
rendered through stories
of his life at Shiprock.
When we first met, I asked
"Where do you sleep at night?"
"Under the stars," he said, flashing
a smile through a few missing teeth.

The days passed. He left for interviews
but never found employment and one
day he said, "I'm going to hitch
my way home to the festival
at Ship Rock. Next year I
want you to come and meet
all my relations. Write down
your address, and I will send
you a map. It's not so far."

In September, I received a note,
and his first map, straightforward:
Denver to Farmington, Farmington
to Ship Rock, 400 miles via US
Highway 285 and US-160W.

His map was precise: his hand-
writing good. He had been
a private in the US Army.
"Ye' Bi' Chei begins 10/5.
There will be a Navajo Food
Competition. Miss Northern
Navajo will be crowned.
The elders will sing and dance.
You can stay at the Farmington
Inn. It's not too far.
Please come."
My work was pressing.
I had a husband and
a child and an old car.
I didn't write back.

The second map came
in September, one year later.

Map2

Following this map will take you far
into the territory of the Navajo Nation
along highway 491, best known
as Route 666 but the name was
changed when people complained
that the number made them feel
uncomfortable, because, you know,
some say it's the number of the beast.
Others say it's a sign from angels
Please, when you come only
travel along this road during
the day. At night it can
become dangerous because
of speeders and drunk drivers.
You are a kind white lady

but you will be in Navajo
territory. Tell anyone who
asks that Nelson Begay
invited you to the festival.

You will pass volcanic
rock formations that
tower above the road.
Beautiful Mountain
and Chuska Mountains
rise in the West, while
the Hogback you'll see
in the East. Do not venture
further from the road, as
these formations are sacred
to my people and off-
limits to the public.
Please come.

That night, as the number 666
flashed in my head I
wondered, was I too focused
on the material plane? Too afraid
to listen to my heart? I tried to
listen but I heard nothing
but drumming.

All night the sound of drums
punctuated my sleep as I traced
my route, faithfully following
the censored mythology
of the long, winding highway.

The years passed and from
time-to-time, I visited
Nelson's maps, with regrets
that I never went to the festival.

At night sometimes I still
can't hear my heart, only
the relentless drumming
and the mythology
of the long, winding highway.

Heinrich Bünting (1545–1606), from *Itinerarium Sacrae Scripturae*, a depiction of the world in the form of a three-leaf clover, symbol of the city of Hanover, with Israel and Jerusalem in the center

VI.

How do we map our lives? It is also called "way finding." A human needs to feel in place. Thematic cartography deconstructs our perceptions of literal maps and speaks to us in powerful ways.

Late Summer Crickets

for Chris Ransick

I walk out of the house
into summer twilight.
Crickets are singing from
the grass, from every tree
and bush, inhabiting
the very air, and I listen,
amazed at the cacophony
of sound, quadraphonic,
filling my head.

I had a friend, a gifted
poet, who told me about
the summer crickets,
and after that, every night
I listened, aware of
being occupied by sound.

I can't bring him back
to tell me how much
it has meant to me--

that he knew this
and so much more—
gardener, brewmeister,
chef, musician, and more,
and then he passed from us.
But the crickets, how they sing.

What a poet can make you
hear what you've never
really truly heard before
offers you gratitude
like you've never felt before,
And that's how it is.
That's how it is.

Are They Just Words?

Om shrim maha lakshmiyei swaha

What is the abundance you seek?
Is it wealth?
A fine automobile?
Health?
Extra-planetary experiences?

When you face insomnia
and heart palpitations
in the wee hours is it best
calmness be your abundance?

Explore: **calm**. late 14c., from Old French
calme "tranquility, quiet," traditionally
from Old Italian *calma*, from Late Latin
cauma "heat of the mid-day sun"
(in Italy, a time when everything rests
and is still), from Greek *kauma* "heat"
(especially of the sun), from *kaiein* "to burn"

Calmness. From 1510s. "quietness, stillness,
tranquility," **Calm** (adj.) + **-ness**

Her panic was gone, leaving calmness in its wake.

Or should you seek to be
abundantly peaceful?

Explore: **peace**. From Middle English *pece*, peas, pees,
from Old French *pais* ("peace"), from Latin *pāx* ("peace"),
from Proto-Indo-European **pak̇-* ("to fasten, stick, place"),
related to Latin *pacīscor* ("agree, stipulate"),
Latin *pangō* ("fasten, fix"); see pact.
Displaced native Middle English *frith*, *frede* ("peace")
(from Old English *friþ*, *frēod* ("peace")),

Middle English *sib, sibbe*("peace") (from Old English *sibb*
("peace, kinship")), Middle English *grith* ("peace, security")
(from Old English *griþ* and Old Norse *grið*), Middle English *saht,*
saught ("peace, reconciliation") (from Old English *seht, sæht*
("peace, pact, agreement")).

Peaceful. From early 14c. "inclined to peace, friendly, pacific."
Peace. From **peace** + **-full**

How **peaceful** she found the phenomena of the lake.

Might serenity be the most sought-after abundance?

Explore: **serenity**. The word "Serenity" is the noun form of the
root word "Serene."
Function: adjective
Etymology (WORD ORIGIN): Middle English, from Latin *serenus*
clear, cloudless, untroubled
1 a : clear and free of storms or unpleasant change <serene
skies> b : shining bright and steady <the moon, serene in glory
-- Alexander Pope>
2 : AUGUST -- used as part of a title <His Serene Highness>
3 : marked by or suggestive of utter calm and unruffled repose or
quietude <a serene smile>
Creating gives birth to serenity.
Words "are in the invisible bag we carry behind us."

I Map the Universe

Galaxies, like many things we map
do not have precise boundaries.
rest of the universe is moving through space.
Who am I to map the Milky Way?
What might our galaxy look like from
an interstellar spaceship including
the distances and positions of more
than eight thousand bright stars, star
clusters, and giant molecular clouds?
Described by the ancients as a river, as milk,
and as a path, among other things, the band
has been visible in the heavens since
Earth first formed.

In daylight, I look up, imagining what is above
me, seeing only a veil of transparent cirrostratus
clouds, fibrous, nearly covering the whole sky.

Death of a House Finch

Well named. They stay close
to the house, singing, close
to the feeder, sometimes quarreling
with another for a perch.
This morning I saw him, lying
on the ground, breathing hard.
I brought him water, then stepped
away, into the shadows of my house,
hoping I wasn't watching him die,
imagining him unfurling his wings
and fluttering up into the sky.
But that wasn't to be as I watched
his last panting breaths and then
saw his legs curled in death
as he melted into the earth, his
scarlet patch defiant, intense,
alive in the morning sunlight.
Small death you think, but death
is real, and death begets beauty

and the sweet contrast
between life and death.
I buried him in a sock
embroidered with animals,
before placing a tiny stone
Buddha at the bottom
to share his sleep.

"Death is the Mother of beauty," Wallace Stevens

Mourning Song

For the animals.
A poster nailed
to a telephone pole.
A cat that will
never be found.
In homage I stopped
by the side of the road,
where a tiny green
bird lay.

I grieve for the falling
leaves, for poets
who died too young.
The house is full
of strange whistles
and thumps.

My heart is screaming
for attention no
one can hear.

The children in cages.
The dark of early afternoon.
Silent snow.
Old blind dogs.
Bad pennies.
Stones with no stories.

Call Everything by Its Right Name

Saturday, June 10, 2017, 95 degrees.
Pastoral, landscape, memory, time.
I am from planet Earth and I contain
the multiplicities of places I have been.
Memory, time, place. A polygon
looks like a broken umbrella.
Raven please bring us light.

In the dark, I polish the stars.
I wonder how they looked
before they were polished.

People take turns reading
Ceprano man. His time?
Thousands of years ago.
North ice caves. Place is also time.

Photographs are absurd abstractions,
sprouting colors never seen in nature.
What is nature? Is it what we think it is?

What is music? Ask Beethoven.
He says, "listen." Still point. No
Fixed point in the world, but ceaseless,
ceaseless metamorphosis and lonely,
lonely cries of the heart.
Terror of the infinite. Greek—
Ἄπειρος *ápeiros*. Everything is generated
from *apeiron* and then it is destroyed
by going back to *apeiron*, according to necessity.

The spring mind, like spring itself, sometimes
grows and sometimes flowers, scenting the air.
Clusters of flowers inhabit the mind, amorphous,
yet resilient to contradiction, contradictory impulses.

Red winged blackbirds are back as well as
assorted characters of death and blight.

In a past life I was an indigo elephant.
I still am in my heart as I channel a higher
indigo chakra to be a super psychic and help
both people and animals, and with practice,
I can contact not only beings in this world,
but beings in other worlds. Supremely
powerful psychic elephant spirit.

The pink moon has come and gone
But last night we saw the strawberry moon.

Luscious

Call everything by its right name.
Know the meaning of the words
you use, but then there is this—
dividing the world into agents
and operations leads to silly questions.

Embrace Tathātā—suchness, best
revealed in the seemingly mundane,
such as watching the wind ripple
through a field of grass.

Mutations

A common housefly develops a third eye
as a result of slipped strand mispairing.
It flies beatifically, making music
with each stroke of its gossamer wings.
A mourning dove breaks from its shell
with a red heart on its chest, beating.

Then on the forehead of a bodhisattva,
a third eye appears and one wonders,
is this a mutation or something
only this vaunted one knows she
possesses? Nevertheless, its reality
cannot be questioned, as seeing
through this mysterious eye,
is like a door opening to reality.

And She Sleeps

I walk down a narrow street in Chitwan,
Nepal, following an elephant carrying
three riders, who laugh uproariously,
enjoying their trip on her back, unaware
of their weight and the day's intense heat.
The Mahout smacks the elephant again
and again with a small stick and
I follow behind until we are close
to the river where the people disembark
on a small step ladder, as the massive
elephant stands compliantly,

I follow until we are next to
the river when soon the Mahout
says "She is girl," and walks
away, leaving me with the elephant
who still bears her worn leather pad.

I stroke her face and soon
she closes her eyes.
I keep stroking her face,
thinking that she is now asleep,
dreading her ride and the next,
and the lash of the stick,
to keep her going, to entertain,
to provide an exotic gift.

A story to take home. "I rode
an elephant."
She sleeps. Her eyes are still
closed. I still stroke her face,
her skin rough as tree bark.
The Mahout directs me to the river
where he takes her to be washed,
and I follow, until I'm up to my knees
in the river, rubbing her with
a stone from head to back to flanks.

Will she dance next? What tricks
other tricks will be required? Or will
she plod along as the hours pass,
living a life of drudgery, beyond
her intelligence, beyond her
desire any longer to stand without
shackles, to be free, wandering
among sweet grasses,
with her herd.
Now, she sleeps.

She Never Knew the Birds Had Carved
a Space in Her Heart

At dawn, she stood in her backyard listening
until the sun rose and dust settled on the silence.
The neighbors who saw her standing there came
to her, concerned about her stillness, she had been
standing alone so long, waiting for the trill
of a bird, the chattering of the chickadees,
the cry of the spotted towhee, coming
through the dawn and the early morning.

She felt wounded by unexplainable love.
The woman now knew that she
had never understood silence.
"Where are the birds?" she asked
the neighbors. "Where are the birdsongs?"
"Migration," said Emma the teacher.
"Migration," Susan the librarian repeated.
"The birds are migrating now," said
Emma, cajoling, and the woman felt
diminished as if she were being coaxed
to understand something unfathomable.
She thanked them and bid them
a good morning. A good day.
Migration. Yes, she said, rueful,
yet finding herself at one with
the birds. "Migration."
Had she ever migrated? Or remained
fixed to a place that nurtured her
and kept her safe?
She imagined their journey
wishing she could migrate
with them, following their songs,
floating among a cloud of downy feathers,
until she arrived with them somewhere
new, where they would sing again
at dawn and she would no longer
have to bear such silence.

Rivers Flow into the Sea

My mind is empty. My heart is full
to overflowing. Beyond dreams
I think of rivers cresting their banks
and hard surf and rip tides challenging
innocent waders.

Rivers flow into the sea. There
is no innocence. People flow
with the water. It is unstoppable,
yet compels us to be one
with this undeniable element
of our being, frightening or strange
when we are immerged, unfolded
in water, as if we had been born
there, and of course we once had
been, beyond our memory, though
some claim to remember that pre-birth
time when some believe they were
safe and secure before they faced
pain for the first time or moments
of infant bliss. Trying to imagine that
time results in desperate yearning until
one says no more! and accommodates
to dailiness, time's ordinary unfolding,
understanding that numbness
is not painful.

Benediction

We went to church every Sunday.
It wasn't an option. My father
made us go. He was the head usher.
A role he bore with too much pride.
My mother and I sat together
sharing a hymnal. My mother
wore a hat, always on Sunday.
I wore my Sunday best, whatever
that was, a dress of course.
Mother's singing one could
say was holy, as she sang
out of faith and love.
My father never joined
us, an usher after he was
no longer needed,
a Christian soldier.
My small brother fidgeted,
bored on the hard pew.
Did we sing together
my mother's favorite
hymn? "What a Friend
We have in Jesus"?
"All our sins and griefs
to bear." An anthem
for my suffering mother
who had little joy
to burn out her pain.
There was the choir
and the long-forgotten
sermon.

Jesus had long ago
not spoken to me.

And, I waited for it:
the Benediction, as if
these were words
for me alone. "May
the Lord bless you
and keep you; the Lord
make his face shine
upon you and be gracious
to you." By then, I knew
these words were not
for me. Not for me as I had
already strayed far from
this faith. No such blessing
would ever comfort me again.
The service ended
and we strayed from
our pews desultoriously,
some of us seeking only
the blessing of Sunday
sunlight.

ELEANOR SWANSON's work is widely published. Awards include an NEA Fellowship and a Colorado Council on the Arts Fellowship. Her first poetry collection, *A Thousand Bonds: Marie Curie and the Discovery of Radium*, was a finalist for the Colorado Book Award, and her second collection of poetry, *Trembling in the Bones—About the Colorado Coal strike of 1913 and the 1914 Ludlow Massacre*—was reissued in 2013 (3: A Taos Press). Her third poetry collection is *Memory's Rooms* (Conundrum Press). She is also a fiction writer. She has published a novel and two collections of short stories. Her second short story collection, *Exiles and Expatriates*, won the 2014 Press Americana Prize. Other awards include first place in the National Writers Union Annual Competition, finalist for the Missouri Review's Larry Levis Editors' Prize, and Nimrod International's Pablo Neruda's Prize. She has a fourth collection of poetry, *Non Finito*, recently published by Fernwood Press.

SHANTI ARTS

NATURE · ART · SPIRIT

Please visit us online
to browse our entire book catalog,
including poetry collections and
non-fiction books on nature, healing,
art, and more.

Also take a look at our highly
regarded art and literary journal,
Still Point Arts Quarterly, a feast for
the eyes and the imagination —
available to download for free.

www.shantiarts.com